lucid living

lucid living

timothy freke

HAY HOUSE

Australia • Canada • Hong Kong • India
South Africa • United Kingdom • United States

Published and distributed in the United Kingdom by:
Hay House UK Ltd, 292B Kensal Rd, London W10 5BE. Tel.: (44) 20
8962 1230; Fax: (44) 20 8962 1239. www.hayhouse.co.uk

A catalogue record for this book is available from the British Library.

This title was previously published by Books for Burning, 2005,
ISBN 978-0-9526-3209-2.

ISBN 978-1-4019-1585-8

Cover photo: Sanvean

Printed and bound in Great Britain by TJ International, Padstow,
Cornwall.

Imagine for a moment you are dreaming. You are completely engrossed in the dramas of your dreamworld when a mysterious stranger appears in your dream. He sidles up to you and softly whispers something extraordinary in your ear: 'Pssst! Wake up. You're dreaming.'

You are disconcerted but keep your cool. You know that the best way to deal with people who are clearly out of the box is to nod politely and hope they will go away.

But the stranger is persistent. 'I know it sounds mad to you right now, but you're dreaming.'

You feel irritated: 'That's absurd!'

The stranger is unperturbed: 'Is it really absurd? Haven't you noticed how full of significant patterns and strange coincidences your experience is? As if there is some hidden meaning? Well, that's because this is a dream.'

You become angry: 'What! Are you saying that this world is just some kind of unreal delusion? I find that offensive. Tell that to all those people who are suffering!'

The stranger is patient: 'Of course this world is real. It is a real dreamworld. Its wonders are truly wonderful and its horrors are truly horrible. I'm not dismissing it. I'm simply pointing out that it's a dream.'

You are confused: 'What do you mean?'

The stranger explains: 'Right now you think you are a person talking to me. But that's just who you temporarily appear to be in this dream. The real you is the dreamer. And this whole dreamworld exists in you.'

You feel stunned: 'Are you asking me to believe that I am imagining talking to you? Surely you are not a product of my imagination?!'

The stranger smiles kindly: 'The person that you seem to be is not imagining this conversation with me, because that person is a part of the dream. But really you are the dreamer who is imagining everything and everyone in this dream. We appear to be separate people having a conversation, but actually we are both the dreamer.'

You begin to panic: 'Now you're freaking me out. I'm losing my hold on who I am.'

The stranger is reassuring: 'Don't worry. You're just beginning to wake up. This is a dream of awakening. It's designed to progressively make you more conscious, until you're conscious enough to realise that you are dreaming.'

You are confused: 'But I don't understand. How do I wake up?'

The stranger looks you straight in the eyes: 'You can wake up any time you want. You simply have to want to wake up more than you fear it. And there is nothing to fear. Waking up feels good. Knowing you are dreaming is the secret of enjoying the dream.'

Your anxiety becomes excitement. You want to wake up. And the more you want to wake up the more you become conscious that you are dreaming. And that feels good. You are no longer frightened of all the terrors that may afflict you in the dream, because you know that the real you is safe. Even if the person you seem to be were to die it would be OK, because actually you are the dreamer.

How marvellous!

Overwhelmed with gratitude you begin to thank the stranger, but he has moved on and is now deep in conversation with someone else, who is looking shocked and intrigued. You call after him: 'What now?'

He turns to you briefly and grins: 'Enjoy the dream. And help everyone else enjoy it as well, because we are all you.'

For a moment you just stand there and let this awesome realisation sink in. Then you notice nearby a number of anxious-looking people hurrying about their business, fully convinced they know exactly who they are and what is going on. You smile to yourself, sidle up to one of them and whisper softly: 'Pssst! Wake up. You're dreaming.'

Wouldn't that be an amazing dream!

But how would you react if this were
to actually happen to you right now?
Because I am the stranger and I want to
make an extraordinary suggestion…

Life is not what it seems.

You're not who you think you are.

Life is like a dream.

And you are the dreamer.

Have you ever been conscious that you were dreaming whilst asleep at night? This is known as 'lucid dreaming'. I want to suggest that it is possible to experience an ultra-awake state I call 'lucid living', in which you are conscious that life is like a dream. But I'm not asking you to just believe me. I want to share with you a way of thinking about life that will wake you up, so that you experience lucid living for yourself.

Lucid living requires a fundamental shift of perspective, comparable to looking at one of those pictures of coloured dots that suddenly turns into a spectacular 3D image. The first such picture I looked at promised me dolphins, but I could see only dots. I didn't know how to make the image come alive. My friends kept assuring me that, if I just stopped concentrating on the dots and focused my eyes on infinity instead, I would definitely see the 3D image. But the more I was reassured, the more irritated I became at my failure. Then suddenly, for a startling moment, the magic happened. Dots became dolphins, leaping lifelike out of the page towards me. And, just as suddenly, they were gone again. Encouraged by my brief success, I kept looking until I gradually got it. Now I can see these 3D images quite easily.

Experiencing lucid living can be like this. At first it sounds ludicrous, but keep looking and eventually you will get it. The trick to viewing a 3D image is to change your visual focus. The trick to experiencing lucid living is to change the way you think. And that is what I am here to help you do. I want to introduce you to a way of thinking about life that will utterly transform your experience of living.

I feel privileged that you have invited me into your mind to share these ideas with you. And I don't want to abuse your hospitality by wasting any of your valuable time. So I've kept things as concise as possible, by distilling down the simple essence of lucid philosophy. But that makes for rich reading, which means this book needs to be savoured, not gulped.

Speed-reading may lead to mental indigestion. The more consciously you read, the more likely you are to experience lucid living.

I am going to lead you through seven powerful insights that will work together to wake you up from the sleeping sickness that keeps you unconscious in the life-dream. Some of these insights are deceptively simple. Some may seem familiar and others may seem weird. But I urge you to approach each insight with an open mind and to give it your undivided attention. If you assume you already understand what an insight means, or you have already decided that it's meaningless nonsense, this will prevent you awakening.

To help you avoid just reading the words and missing the meaning of each insight, I am going to suggest you perform a number of philosophical experiments. In these experiments I will talk you into experiencing lucid living by posing questions and then presenting my answers. Take the time to perform each experiment yourself and see if my answers also work for you. Make sure you actually do this. Otherwise lucid living will remain just a bizarre idea.

Before we embark on our philosophical adventure, let me make something very clear. When I compare life to a dream I do not mean to denigrate it as some sort of meaningless fantasy. Life is too wonderful to be called an 'illusion', unless we whisper the word in amazement, as we might when witnessing the most astonishing magic trick. What could be more magnificent than this glorious universe, in all its multifarious extravagance? Its awesome vastness and delicate detail. Its impersonal precision and intimate intensity. Its harsh necessities and lush sensuality. This dream of life is truly marvellous.

This is a little book with grand aspirations.
It will take you less than an hour to read, but
it could change your life for good.

I urge you to read it straight through,
because you're more likely to reach a
philosophical climax if you take it all at once.
Especially if it's your first time.

I can't promise to wake you up. Lucid living is like falling in love. It happens when it happens. You can't force it and you can't prevent it.

But I can take you on a blind date with some extremely bold and beautiful ideas. And – you never know – it might be the beginning of something big!

So let me introduce our first insight…

life is a mystery

The idea that life is like a dream seems preposterous because we presume we are already wide awake. But most of the time we are so unconscious we don't even notice the most obvious thing about existence: it is an enigma of mind-boggling enormity. Life is the mother of all mysteries – quite literally! Yet we are normally so asleep that we manage to go about our daily business as if being alive was nothing remarkable.

Join me in a philosophical experiment and let's examine the human predicament…

Here we are.

Meeting in this perpetual moment we call 'now'.

Participants in this bizarre business we call 'life'.

Awaiting the inevitable ending we call 'death'.

What's it all about?!

Do you know?

Does anyone really know?

People travel all over the world in search of mysteries and miracles, but what could be more mysterious and miraculous than life itself?

Not just what it is, but that it is at all!

When the Hubble telescope was focused on the night sky each tiny black dot revealed dozens of galaxies, with each galaxy containing millions of stars!

The universe is too immense to imagine and infinitely mysterious. And if you live to be 80 years old you will have just 4000 weeks in which to understand it.

That puts things in perspective, don't you think?

Our predicament is so profoundly puzzling, it is astonishing that we aren't permanently perplexed.

Most of us rush around as if there is no more to life than making a living and not thinking about dying.

We never stop to wonder.

We behave as if we know exactly what life is all about, even though secretly we know we don't.

It is as if we are mesmerised by our assumptions about life into a sort of semi-conscious trance, which anaesthetises us to the awesome strangeness of existence.

That is until the bubble bursts and we unexpectedly wake up.

It may be an encounter with death that jolts us back to life. Or the bewildering bliss of falling in love. Or a simple shaft of sunlight through a window.

Whatever form the wake-up call takes, for a marvellous moment we shake off the numbness we call 'normality' and find ourselves immersed in overwhelming, unfathomable, breathtaking mystery.

Have you ever had an experience like this?

Be conscious of the mystery of existence right now.

The fact that we normally take life for granted, when it is actually so utterly mysterious, shows how unconscious we usually are.

We are so wrapped up in our opinions about life that we mistake our own make-believe world for reality – just as when we are dreaming.

Becoming conscious of the mystery of existence is like waking up from a dream.

If you're feeling mystified, that's good, because it means you're ready for our second insight…

now is all you know

When we are asleep and dreaming, things are not what they seem. We are so engrossed in our imagination that we don't realise we are dreaming. We believe we know what is going on, but really we don't. I want to suggest that life is like a dream. And that right now we are so engrossed in the life-dream we don't realise we are dreaming. We believe we know what is going on, but really we don't.

Most of us are so completely certain of our everyday understanding of life that this seems ridiculous. But are we right to be so certain? I don't think so. I want to suggest that all we actually know for sure is what we are experiencing right now. And if we really pay attention to our experience of this moment we will discover that life is like a dream.

Join me in another philosophical experiment and let's think it through together…

To most people the idea that life is like a dream is ludicrous. I'm a philosopher, not an evangelist, so I am all in favour of giving new ideas a sceptical reception.

But I am also in favour of adopting the same sceptical attitude towards our familiar ideas.

Are you open to the possibility that your present understanding of life could be mistaken?

Is there actually anything about which you can be absolutely certain?

Can you be certain of the common-sense understanding of reality taken for granted by most people in our culture?

I don't think so.

History shows that today's sensible certainties soon become tomorrow's silly superstitions. We look back at many of the beliefs of our ancestors and find them crazy and amusing. Isn't it possible that our descendants will look back at our present cultural assumptions and find them equally crazy and amusing?

Can you be certain of your own personal convictions?

I don't think so.

Haven't you often felt completely sure about something, only to later decide that you were wrong? Isn't it possible you will discover your present beliefs are also wrong?

Are you with me?

You can doubt all the beliefs that you have taken on trust from other people, because you don't know them to be true for yourself.

Do you agree?

You can doubt all beliefs that are based on your memories of the past, because memory is fallible.

That's a full-on thought, but it's right, isn't it?

Is there anything about which you can be absolutely certain?

Yes.

You are experiencing something right now.

That's indisputably true, isn't it?

Your experience of this moment is not a belief that can be questioned. It is a self-evident certainty.

Your experience of this moment is all you can be absolutely sure of.

So the only way to really understand life is to examine your own immediate experience of living.

Isn't that an empowering realisation!

If you want to know what is going on, you can't rely on me or anyone else to tell you.

You must find out for yourself by paying attention to what you are experiencing right now.

And – I want to suggest – if you do become more conscious of this present moment, you will discover that life is like a dream.

OK so far? Because from here it's a bit of a philosophical roller-coaster ride. Hang on tight. Or better still, let go completely! Because we are going to be moving fast.

Lucid living isn't believing the theory that life is like a dream. It is directly experiencing the dream-like nature of reality in this present moment.

I want to point out some clues which suggest life is like a dream, for you to check out for yourself in your own immediate experience.

The first clue is our next insight. But be prepared. It challenges our most basic assumption about who we are…

you are not a person

When you are dreaming you appear to be a character within the dream. But this is only your 'apparent identity'. It is not who you really are. Actually you are awareness which is dreaming the dream. This is your 'essential identity'. I am suggesting that life is like a dream. Right now you appear to be a person in the life-dream. But this is only your apparent identity, it is not who you really are. Your essential identity is much less concrete and much more mysterious. You are awareness which is witnessing the life-dream.

If you are willing to let go of the assumption that you are a person – just as an experiment – I will point out who you really are…

Examine the reality of this present moment.

You are experiencing something right now.

That's obvious, right?

So you are an experiencer of experiences.

That's a weird way of seeing yourself, but it's clearly true, isn't it?

Try it out.

Be an experiencer of experiences.

Be awareness witnessing all that is happening right now.

Common sense, of course, says you are a person. But even in everyday speech we say 'I have a body,' not 'I am a body.' And we talk of 'my mind' as if the mind is something we possess, not something we are.

What is this mysterious 'I' which is not the body or mind?

It is awareness which witnesses the body and mind.

Can you get that?

Over your lifetime your body has aged and your mind has matured, but don't you feel as if something has remained the same?

*Isn't the essential you no different now
from when you were younger?*

*What is this essential you that is constant
and enduring?*

It is awareness.

*Awareness is the constant background of
all your experiences.*

*Awareness is the unchanging witness of all
that changes.*

*Awareness is a perpetual presence that is
always present.*

Do you agree?

Right now you are awareness witnessing a flow of experiences. This is your permanent essential identity.

Within the flow of experiences you appear to be a particular person. This is your ever-changing apparent identity.

Your apparent identity is not who you are. It is who you temporarily appear to be.

This will become obvious if you consider your daily experience of waking, dreaming and deep sleep.

When you are asleep and dreaming, the person you presently appear to be disappears from awareness and you appear to be a different person in a different dreamworld.

Your essential identity as awareness remains forever the same, but your apparent identity is completely transformed every night.

Indeed, in deep sleep your apparent identity disappears altogether! Because when awareness is unconscious you don't appear to exist at all.

Common sense says that you are a body within which awareness comes and goes.

But in your own experience you are awareness within which the body comes and goes!

That's an outrageous thought, but it's right, isn't it?

Whilst you are dreaming, your dreamworld seems very real – sometimes terrifyingly so – and you believe you are the person you appear to be in the dream.

But when you dream lucidly, you know that this isn't who you really are, because you know you are the dreamer witnessing the dream.

If you want to live lucidly, stop believing you are the person you appear to be right now.

Be awareness witnessing this ever-changing moment.

How are you doing? Grasping unfamiliar ideas can be a bit like trying to hold onto the soap in the bath, so take a mental breather if you need one.

But not too long, because we're working towards a reality-shift which will – quite literally – turn the world inside-out. And that will require plenty of philosophical momentum.

OK. Ready to play? Insight number four is…

the world exists in you

When you dream you appear to be a dream-persona in a dreamworld, but actually you are awareness and the dreamworld exists within you. In the same way right now you appear to be a person in the life-dream, but actually you are awareness and the life-dream exists within you.

Let's look...

Right now you are experiencing your thoughts and the world of the senses.

Do you agree?

We usually think of our thoughts as existing within awareness and the world as existing independently of awareness. But is that right?

If you pay attention to what is happening right now you will see that you experience the world as a series of sensations: visual images, tactile feelings, background sounds, ambient aromas.

And sensations exist within awareness, don't they?

Everything you are aware of exists within awareness, otherwise you wouldn't be aware of it!

So what is awareness?

Awareness isn't something within your experience. It is an emptiness that contains all you are experiencing.

That's right, isn't it?

Become conscious of yourself as a spacious emptiness within which everything you are experiencing right now exists.

These printed words you are reading on this page exist within awareness.

These ideas reverberating in your mind exist within awareness.

All you see and hear and touch and imagine exists within awareness.

Your body exists within awareness.

The world exists within awareness.

You may appear to be a physical body in the world, but actually you are awareness and the world exists in you.

If that comes as a shock – there's more.

You don't exist in time!

Look for yourself right now.

Time is the perpetual flow of ever-changing appearances which awareness witnesses.

Time exists within awareness.

Awareness is outside time.

You are timeless awareness dreaming itself to be a person in time. Far out!

Are you suffering from philosophical vertigo?

Well, stay steady. Because our fifth insight is
a very big idea indeed...

all is one

When we dream we appear to be one of many characters in our dream-drama. But actually everyone and everything is being imagined by one dreaming awareness. It is the same right now. We appear to be many separate individuals. But actually we are all different characters in the life-dream that is being dreamt by the one life-dreamer. And that's who we really are. We are one awareness dreaming itself to be many individuals in the life-dream.

Take a look...

As a person you have different mental and physical characteristics to me.

Do you agree?

Your apparent identity is distinct from my apparent identity.

But is your essential identity as awareness distinct from my essential identity as awareness?

No.

As awareness you are a permanent witnessing presence. And as awareness so am I.

As awareness you are not in space or time. And as awareness neither am I.

As awareness we are indistinguishable.

We appear to be different, but essentially we are the same.

That's right, isn't it?

We share our essential identity as awareness in common.

As awareness we are all one.

We are one awareness dreaming itself to be many different personas in the life-dream.

We are one awareness experiencing the life-dream from the different perspectives of these different personas.

That's massive!

Are you enjoying the ride?

Don't be surprised to feel like you're in *The Matrix* or *Alice Through the Looking Glass*. Because in a way you are. Except the life story is even more full of ironic twists.

Lucid living is realising you are both the hero of your particular story and the imagination which is conceiving the whole cosmic drama.

It is understanding our sixth insight…

you are a paradox

When you dream you are both the source of the dream and a character within the dream. Your identity is inherently paradoxical. In the same way your identity right now is also inherently paradoxical. You are both the source of the life-dream and a character within it. You are the life-dreamer imagining yourself to be a particular person in the life-dream. Whilst you identify exclusively with your life-persona you will remain unconsciously engrossed in the life-dream. Lucid living happens when you become conscious of both poles of your paradoxical nature.

Give it a go...

You appear to be a body in the world.

Now flip it around.

You are awareness and the world exists in you.

Try it again.

You appear to be a person in time.

Flip it around.

You are a permanent presence witnessing an ever-changing flow of appearances.

Try it again.

You appear to be a separate individual.

Flip it around.

You are the life-dreamer experiencing existence from a particular point of view.

One more time.

You appear to be a character in the life-dream.

Flip it around.

You are the life-dreamer and everything is you.

Lucid living is consciously being all that you are.

Waking up to your essential identity
as awareness doesn't negate your
individuality. Quite the opposite.

Lucid living is understanding just how
important your individuality is. Because
it is by dreaming itself to be you as an
individual that the life-dreamer is able to
experience the life-dream.

Lucid living is feeling truly empowered
as a person. Because you know that the
creative energy of the whole universe is
propelling you forward in your life.

Lucid living doesn't deny the delights and
dramas of everyday existence. It charges
life with new significance and meaning.

Everything you experience is a manifestation of your essential nature. So everything is showing you something about who you are – like a dream.

You are continually dreaming up new situations that give you the opportunity to become more conscious.

Lucid living is wholeheartedly engaging with ordinary life as an epic adventure of awakening.

Lucid living isn't withdrawing into some detached state of enlightenment. It is enjoying an exhilarating state of enlivenment!

We have travelled a huge distance in a short time, so don't be surprised if you feel a little dizzy with philosophical jet lag.

Yet, here we are, exactly where we started. Conscious of this present moment.

Nothing has changed. Yet everything has changed. Because waking up fundamentally transforms how it feels to be a person in the life-dream.

Which brings us to the climax of our philosophical reality-check and our seventh insight…

being one is loving all

What is love? We love someone when we are so close we know we are not separate. Love is what we feel when we realise we are one.

Normally we presume we are just the person we appear to be, so we feel connected to those we embrace within our limited sense of who we are, such as our friends and family. We are hostile to those who threaten our personal self, and indifferent to everyone else.

Our loving stops where our sense of self ceases. But when we realise we are everyone and everything, we find ourselves intimately connected to everyone and everything. When we know that all is one, we experience love without limits.

Check it out…

Meet me in this moment.

These words are reaching through time and space, connecting us together.

I am conscious of you reading. Are you conscious of me writing?

Here we are.

The one life-dreamer meeting itself in different forms.

Apparently separate. Essentially the same.

Are you with me?

How does it feel to realise that we are not separate?

How does it feel to be one with everyone and everything?

For me it is an experience of communion and compassion.

Being one with all, I am in love with all.

When I wake up to oneness I feel a limitless love which is so deep and poignant that it embraces life in all its ecstasy and agony.

I share in our collective joy and suffering.

And I find my selfish preoccupations are replaced by a longing for everyone to love living.

When I know I am the life-dreamer I want to enjoy the life-dream in all my many disguises.

I want to alleviate our collective distress so that we can celebrate the miracle of existence together – without fear, oppression and hardship.

Don't you also want that?

Since time immemorial wise men and women have been assuring us that love is the only solution to our problems. And they are right.

Only love can heal the divisions between us, because love is the realisation that we are one.

When we assume we are just separate individuals we act in our limited self-interest, regardless of the suffering we may cause others.

The illusion of separateness leads to selfishness and suffering.

But becoming conscious of the reality of oneness leads to the selfless desire to end all suffering and create universal wellbeing.

When we realise separateness is an illusion we understand that conflict is never between us and them, but always us against us.

This realisation has huge implications.

It means harming someone else is just hurting ourselves.

It means revenge – even against the most hideous of criminals – is hurting ourselves again.

It means war – no matter how righteous – is grotesque self-mutilation.

Think of all the needless suffering we are causing ourselves through our mistaken belief that we are separate.

Now imagine how easily we could utterly transform our collective experience of life if we simply lived lucidly in love with all.

Imagine for a moment how good the life-dream could be if we could just wake up!

Lucid living is the simple secret of transforming the life-dream from a nightmare of separateness into the joyous celebration of existence we want it to be.

I am writing these words to you because I want us to wake up.

I see what a wonder you are.

You are infinite potential playing at being a person.

You are the mystery of life made manifest.

I celebrate you.

You are different from me and yet we are one.

And it is only because we are both separate and the same that we can love one another.

That's beautiful!

I want you to see yourself as I see you,
so that we can help each other enjoy this
great dream of awakening.

So that we can inspire each other when we
feel lucid and in love.

And comfort each other when we feel lost
and alone.

So that we can walk each other home.

So that when I become engrossed in the
collective coma we mistake for real life,
you can remind me to live lucidly.

You may be that kind stranger who will
whisper softly...

wake up

The Alliance for Lucid Living

The ALL is a worldwide alliance of individuals who share a passion for the experience of lucid living.

The ALL aims to alleviate the suffering caused by the illusion of separateness by promoting our collective awakening to oneness and love.

Connect with other people who are awakening and receive information about Tim Freke's stand-up philosophy shows and experiential seminars by becoming part of the ALL at **www.timothyfreke.com**

This book would not exist without the wisdom, talents and generosity of:

Deborah O'Shea Freke, Anthony Taylor, Theo Simon, Sean Reynolds, Angie Hayward, Des Rice, Ellen Freke, Peter Gandy, John Lenker, Sanvean, Gower Preston, Chloe White and Susan Mears.

Thank you. I love you.

Tim Freke is a 'stand-up philosopher' and bestselling author. He is a passionate voice for our collective awakening and is frequently featured in the media internationally. His books, CDs and live performances have inspired many thousands of people throughout the world. In his life-changing seminars he shares simple practical techniques to help participants experience lucid living for themselves. To find out more and watch Tim in action visit **www.timothyfreke.com**